To
....

From
....

Compiled by Andrea Skevington
Illustrations copyright © 2004 The Wright Sisters
This edition copyright © 2004 Lion Hudson

A Lion Book
an imprint of
Lion Hudson plc
Mayfield House, 256 Banbury Road,
Oxford OX2 7DH, England
www.lionhudson.com
ISBN 0 7459 5163 5

First edition 2004
1 3 5 7 9 10 8 6 4 2 0

Acknowledgments

Pages 20, 32, 36, 72, 77: Proverbs 17:17, Ecclesiastes 4:9–10, Genesis 31:49, Proverbs 17:14,
Philemon 22, from the *Holy Bible, New International Version*, copyright © 1973, 1978, 1984
International Bible Society. Used by permission of Zondervan and Hodder & Stoughton Limited.
All rights reserved. The 'NIV' and 'New International Version' trademarks are registered in the
United States Patent and Trademark Office by International Bible Society. Use of either trademark
requires the permission of International Bible Society. UK trademark number 1448790. Page 88:
Matthew 5:9, from The Message. Copyright © 1993, 1994, 1995, 1996, 2000, 2001, 2002. Used by
permission of NavPress Publishing Group. Every effort has been made to trace and acknowledge
copyright holders of all the quotations in this book. We apologize for any errors or omissions that
may remain, and would ask those concerned to contact the publishers, who will ensure that full
acknowledgment is made in the future.

A catalogue record for this book is available
from the British Library

Typeset in 16/22 Aunt Mildred
Printed and bound in Singapore

friendship

Compiled by
Andrea Skevington
Illustrated by
The Wright Sisters

A LION BOOK

Friendship...

it's what everyone's looking for!

This is a gift book with
huge appeal across a variety of
different occasions. Through a
selection of tips and quotations
about life and living it looks at
what friendship is, why it's so
important and how we can find it.

Helpful thoughts on living life combined with heartwarming illustrations make this a book that's hard to resist.

1

Friendship is...
sharing hopes
and dreams

We are each of us angels with
only one wing; and we can only fly
by embracing one another.

Luciano de Crescenzo

At the touch of love, everyone becomes a poet.

Plato

Some of the most rewarding and
beautiful moments of a friendship happen
in the unforeseen open spaces between
planned activities. It is important that
you allow these spaces to exist.

Christine Leefeldt

2

Friendship is...

having fun

All who would win joy must share it;

happiness was born a twin.

Lord Byron

There is no beautifier of complexion,

or form, or behaviour, like the wish to

scatter joy and not pain around us.

Ralph Waldo Emerson

Every time you smile at someone,

it is an action of love, a gift to that person,

a beautiful thing.

Mother Teresa of Calcutta

3

Friendship is...

sharing tears

Real friendship is shown in times of trouble;

prosperity is full of friends.

Ralph Waldo Emerson

A friend loves at all times,

and a brother is born for adversity.

The Bible

True friendship multiplies the good
in life and divides its evils. Strive to
have friends, for life without friends is
like life on a desert island… To find one
real friend in a lifetime is good fortune;
to keep him is a blessing.

Baltasar Gracian

Friendship is...
being quiet together

The real test of friendship is:
Can you literally do nothing with the
other person? Can you enjoy together
those moments of life that are utterly simple?
They are the moments people look back on
at the end of life and number as their
most sacred experiences.

Eugene Kennedy

Sometimes being a friend

means mastering the art of timing.

There is a time for silence.

Gloria Naylor

Your very silence shows you agree.

Euripides

5

Friendship is...

going for a walk

Don't walk in front of me, because
I may not follow. Don't walk behind me,
because I may not lead. Just walk
beside me and be my friend.

Albert Camus

Everywhere is walking distance
if you have the time.

Anon

Life's truest happiness is found in
friendships we make along the way.

Steven Wright

6

Friendship is...
doing things
together

Two are better than one, because they
have a good return for their work: if one
falls down, his friend can help him up.

The Bible

Coming together is a beginning,
staying together is progress,
working together is success.

Henry Ford

To like and dislike the same things,

that is indeed true friendship.

Sallust

7

Friendship is...
being friends apart

The road to a friend's house is never long.

Danish proverb

May the Lord keep watch between you
and me when we are away from each other.

The Bible

Don't be dismayed at goodbyes.
A farewell is necessary before you
can meet again. And meeting again,
after moments or lifetimes,
is certain for those who are friends.

Richard Bach

8

Friendship is...
when someone has
known you for years

Wishing to be friends is quick work,
but friendship is slow-ripening fruit.

Aristotle

For believe me, in this world which
is ever slipping from under our feet,
it is the prerogative of friendship to
grow old with one's friends.

Arthur S. Hardy

The greatest happiness of life is

the conviction that we are loved –

loved for ourselves, or rather, loved

in spite of ourselves.

Victor Hugo

9

Friendship is...
when someone you've
just met thinks like you

Friendship is born at the moment when
one person says to another, 'What! You too?
I thought that no one but myself...'

C.S. Lewis

Never refuse any advance of friendship,
for if nine out of ten bring you nothing,
one alone may repay you.

Madame de Tencin

Depth of friendship does not depend on
length of acquaintance.

Rabindranath Tagore

Friendship is...

supporting each other

The glory of friendship is not the
outstretched hand, nor the kindly smile...
it's the spiritual inspiration that comes
to one when he discovers that someone else
believes in him and is willing to trust him
with his friendship.

Ralph Waldo Emerson

Live so that your friends can defend you
but never have to.

Arnold H. Glasgow

A blessed thing it is for any man or
woman to have a friend, one human soul
whom we can trust utterly, who knows
the best and worst of us, and who loves us
in spite of all our faults.

Charles Kingsley

11

Friendship is...
helping each other

When someone allows you to bear his burdens,
you have found deep friendship.

Anon

The finest kind of friendship is between
people who expect a great deal of each other,
but never ask it.

Sylvia Bremer

We secure our friends not by accepting
favours but by doing them.

Thucydides

Do not protect yourself by a fence,
but rather by your friends.

Czech proverb

Friendship is...

valuing each other

If we would build on a sure foundation
in friendship, we must love friends for
their sake rather than for our own.

Charlotte Brontë

I awoke this morning with devout
thanksgiving for my friends, the old
and the new.

Ralph Waldo Emerson

True friendship is seen through the heart,
not through the eyes.

Anon

'Tis the privilege of friendship to talk nonsense,
and have her nonsense respected.

Charles Lamb

13

Friendship is...

giving

May no gift be too small to give, nor
too simple to receive, which is wrapped
in thoughtfulness, and tied with love.

L.O. Baird

What brings joy to the heart is not
so much the friend's gift as the friend's love.

St Aelred of Rievaulx

Remember, the greatest gift is not found
in a store nor under a tree, but in the
hearts of true friends.

Cindy Lew

If instead of a gem, or even a flower,
we should cast the gift of a loving thought
into the heart of a friend, that would
be giving as the angels give.

George Macdonald

14

Friendship is...
knowing when
to offer advice

A friend encourages your dreams and
offers advice – but when you don't follow it,
they still respect and love you.

Doris Wild Helmering

Friendship will not stand the strain of
very much good advice for very long.

Robert Lynd

It is one of the severest tests of friendship
to tell your friend his faults. So to love
a man that you cannot bear to see a stain
upon him, and to speak painful truth
through loving words, that is friendship.

Henry Ward Beecher

15

Friendship is...
listening

One of the most beautiful qualities
of true friendship is to understand
and to be understood.

Seneca

There was a definite process
by which one made people into friends,
and it involved talking to them and
listening to them for hours at a time.

Rebecca West

Listening is a magnetic and strange thing, a creative force. The friends who listen to us are the ones we move toward. When we are listened to, it creates us, makes us unfold and expand.

Karl Menninger

16

♥

Friendship is...
saying sorry
and forgiving

'Tis the most tender part of love,

each other to forgive.

John Sheffield

Starting a quarrel is like breaching a dam;

so drop the matter before a dispute breaks out.

The Bible

Anger makes you smaller, while forgiveness

forces you to grow beyond what you were.

Cherie Carter-Scott

Holding on to anger, resentment and
hurt only gives you tense muscles, a headache
and a sore jaw from clenching your teeth.
Forgiveness gives you back the laughter
and the lightness in your life.

Joan Lunden

Friendship is...
welcoming

Hospitality should have no other
nature than love.

Henrietta Mears

I had three chairs in my house: one for solitude,
two for friendship, three for society.

Henry David Thoreau

The ornament of a house is the friends
who frequent it.

Ralph Waldo Emerson

And one thing more: prepare a guest room for me, because I hope to be restored to you in answer to your prayers.

The Bible

18

Friendship is...

always being there

A friend drops their plans when you're in trouble, shares joy in your accomplishments, feels sad when you're in pain.

Doris Wild Helmering

Love seeketh not itself to please,
Nor for itself hath any care,
But for another gives its ease,
And builds a heaven in hell's despair.

William Blake

It's the friends you can call up
at four a.m. that matter.

Marlene Dietrich

19

Friendship is...

not forgetting

It is wise to apply the oil of refined politeness
to the mechanisms of friendship.

Colette

Friendship is a living thing that lasts
only as long as it is nourished with kindness,
empathy and understanding.

Anon

Friendship consists of forgetting
what one gives, and remembering what
one receives.

Alexandre Dumas

What do we live for if not to make life
less difficult for each other?

George Eliot

20

Friendship is...
encouraging each other

You're blessed when you can show people
how to cooperate instead of compete or fight.
That's when you discover who you really are,
and your place in God's family.

The Bible

Treat your friends as you do your pictures,
and place them in their best light.

Jennie Jerome Churchill

The essence of true friendship is to make allowances for another's little lapses.

David Storey

21

Friendship is...
a blessing

The most important thing in life is to learn
how to give out love, and to let it come in.

Morrie Schwartz

No love, no friendship, can cross the path
of our destiny without leaving some mark
on it for ever.

François Mauriac

The greatest healing therapy is

friendship and love.

Hubert H. Humphrey

Living is having ups and downs and

sharing them with friends.

Trey Parker and Matt Stone